MW00586712

The Maybe-Bird
Jennifer Elise Foerster

The Song Cave

The Song Cave
www.the-song-cave.com
© Jennifer Elise Foerster, 2022

Design and layout by Janet Evans-Scanlon

ISBN: 978-1-7372775-5-2
Library of Congress Control Number: 2022934609

FIRST EDITION

Contents

Nakonakv vcakayis. Hvse ah-ossan
uehvtke rakko tempen vlakis.
Vcekelliyat, yopvn ē-oh-hecis:
Nake vcvhakat, cvtorofv vnsekos.

Sixteen Shadows

The people believed in a future
     with her face—
             concealed
     her seeds
       stars' dull hatchets
       behind the black bark of the moon—
and the whole forest grew
       when they uttered
the ancestors' old notion
         that those who have been buried
               with a little honey
    after marshaling a mournful sound
         thrown in circular waves to the west
can appropriate similar words
     for *Creek*, like
         rattle-wing—
   the flower that expresses the fruit.

I am told heaven is already visible
in the white woods
but I see nothing.

The river was impassable for days.

Encamped near a fish-bitten bank
I found a violin,
      my skull's brass rattle,
           cracked water moccasin
               yellowed from the sun.

I had rendered my provisions—
      two rows of teeth,
          a small knot of fire,
      sugar, keg, hatchet,
        grass—

to sleep in the pines,
        let slip my raft
as if from the ribs of a woman
      whose name I forgot
         and regretted ever since.

There should have been no suffering

    on the rock, stiff fields

        received no children

      no vestiges of corn

    He hath hidden the sun

  in new lands

      a hive

        dislodged from thickets

          nature's antiquary

    bearskin, grain, gun

            What art

should be assembled through such a scene—

      black creek, rusted pine

        a people's baggage

          thrown onto their graves

On the bank of the interior
he anchors in the light of the palms—
        orange illume, lemon, lapis lazuli.

He searches the harbor's slight
movements of time—
        peoples' plumed faces,
                current-drowned stones.

Circle south the canoes
    who go in his name—

        he, with the lightwood,
        who never once turned around
        as they cut off the body—his head
                of gold and tempests
                        hollow in the sand.

I, however, was saved a dance—
        fruit for purchase, fertile.

The whips were weak
without horsemen—

        those hammering hours,
                copper instruments of wind.

By his hand
I received light slowly

glad enough to pass the day
with bright misfortune—

a cloak of swans,
the moon's fine clothing
being blown away.

Possessed by temper's
      curl and stream
           I trace your deluge

over rolling country,
      take pictures in the rain
           of beasts that live on smoke.

I tire of the intoxication
      of reason, its angel crowing,
           pitched over branches.

I cannot language the tree
      or point out the sun's
           strange amulets.

Enchanted, the heart
      is at liberty
           to ruin itself.

Nature will bring all
      under the great wave
           by degrees.

Exhausted from the violent order of hours
we took shelter in the country of Coosa—
a deserted village with thin deer, flint roads.

We learned to navigate painted margins,
fence the fields, plant stones,
make of nothing bread enough,

did not resist the music of the swamp,
old dances raising the river's black dress,
her perfumed cane, rum-skinned fruit—

in the mouth of March
we were swimming in flowers

and lived in this manner
without men or wars
on the left banks of the earth.

The orchestra of bees in the grove sounds
nothing like the alphabet we used to speak.

   We have tried the only antidote
rattling in the gulley—

         the bite of the industrious sovereign—
            Serpentaria americana.

The delicate task of extracting
         those primitive sores—

               warm fat seeds
         blazing beneath our feet—

may depend upon certain
         bodies of rain or
               water spirits—

                  vain musicians of time
                     and complaint.

I thought it enough

for my ration—

        three cells of salt.

          Serrated fire.

      Dogwood on a bluff.

The sickness from its bark—

          a virtue for the solitary

riding a lone corner of the nation

People used to say, to expel the honeyed
thorn of that cancer, one must keep
a lung of briars, the grace to last
through anxious rain, and purpose,
the burn of the panther's mouth—

        that those weary of fighting
                have never seen the captives of God.

After the disease was brought to the nation,
we folded our fish nets, deerskins, hands,
our flutes and arrows rent in pieces.

Long governed by destruction,
we were a sovereign madness
piloting night's imperial bowels,
scraping stiff canoes through the streets.

We had little idea of the rushing effect—
the scald of rattlesnake weather,
how ash would thread raw
wounds into blankets.

People used to say, a great way off
is the dominion of the north,
a vast beach painted black
where people live in bolts of trees
stealing prickly trinkets of lightning.

Should their world
be a patient country, as the sea
to its shawl of crimson horses.

The messenger follows its own devices
guided by fragrance of grass
laced through endless blazes.

I saw nothing—a burnt-out passage,
deserted houses, barren stone,

a series of flame-fringed ridges—
trackless geography awash in pitch.

What conceit, drawn
with an American camera—

the scenery of another epoch's
slender pines seemed to rest
as on a robe of marten skins.

Here you are, deception,
      worn out but growing swiftly

      at liberty in all seasons
to sail through other people's raptures.

Rising at midnight
      he draws several white doors—

earth mounds, conic and oblong.

      His line of sight
industrious for simplicity—

        wind
            wheeling in a limestone quarry

black hills in shadow

        the right angles of fire.

    Consumed by him, I forget

      thirst.

        Rage.

           What was killing us.

But the country was rich
    with mischief.

Hogs and horses
freezing in the night
devoured their people.

They dug a pit
    for newcomers,

burned the remaining pine.

I thought it artificial,
the civilized region—
a black wolf in bark skins.

The river continues
in scale and shell
to answer my wild curiosity
by presenting similar creatures
who pass through this gorge—

alligators of the low ponds
eye me intently

as far as I am from being
useful to the soil
or dead in their holes.

The war appeared to be coming
to an end.

The no-name people not yet taken
left their crops for summer's drought.

A bow in the mouth, they passed unseen,
forded the river for rock trout, crystals,
the eastward hillside dense with vines.

Eyeing the sunrise, they travelled for days,
and lost in the reeds, heard everything—

earthworms, thunder,
yesterday's moss,

the patient banks of morning.

No traces of women
in the maize. The children—
hieroglyphics inscribed by teeth
on the side of the streaming river.

I accompanied the settlers
for the whole journey.

To walk leisurely
over never-ending grass—
that was my punishment.

Here is a field of smoke to sow

    a stone

        a rose

     a tree

        a rope.

The earth suspends its one

           inky eye.

Here is an arrow

       hands

    a face.

Here are manners: be

    careful

        contained. O nervous

      ornamental nation—

for all improvements

       be happy.

Farewell

rain. Farewell

night.

In times of floods

we all fall from flight.

Note:

This series repurposes language from eight texts written by explorers or Indian Agents to Creek County from 1527 to 1828. The process involved cutting, erasing, and rearranging language, which resulted in a series of text-quilts. The following eight texts were used:

Alvar Nunez Cabeza De Vaca, *Adventures in the Unknown Interior of America, First Lieutenant in* the *Nárvez Expedition, 1527-36*

Thomas Nairne, *Nairne's Muskhogean Journals: The 1708 Expedition to the Mississippi River*

John Pope, *A Tour Through the Southern and Western Territories of the United States of North-America: the Spanish Dominions of the Mississippi, and the Floridas; the Country of the Creek Nations; and Many Uninhabited Parts* (1792)

George Stiggins, *Creek Indian History: A Historical Narrative of the Genealogy, Traditions and Downfall of the Ispocoga or Creek Indian Tribe of Indians by One of the Tribe, George Stiggins (1788-1845)*

Benjamin Hawkins, *The Collected Works of Benjamin Hawkins, 1796-1810*

Basil Hall, *Travels in North American in the years 1827 and 1828*

Ethan Allen Hitchcock, *A Traveler in Indian Territory: The Journal of Ethan Allen Hitchcock* (1842)

William Bartram. *Travels of William Bartram, edited by Mark Van Doren.* Dover Editions, 1955.

MVSKOKE EMPONAKVN
KERRETV

Estvmimvn areckv? Hvsse. Hvrēssē.

Estvmimvn vlakeckv? Tvstvnvke. Kolaswv.

Totkv. Wakv pesē. Hoktē. Hopuewv.

Torwv. Vnhesse. Mekko. Eto.

Eto hacohakat. Eto-tale.

Mekko hacohakat. Efv hacohakat.

Vfopken wakkvs. Nenucen ohwakkvs.

Fvccv omv? Nettv em ehaketv.

Catv. 'Fv hoktē. Nokose.

Pocoswv.

Epesē. Coksakkv. Etalwa.

Eslafkv.

Vyomockusan em vtēkēn vlakis.

Fo encvmpē.

Where are you going? The Sun. The Moon

Where did you come from? Warrior. Star.

Fire. Milk. A Woman. Child.

Eye. My Friend. King. The tree.

Mad Lightwood. Dry pine.

Mad king. Mad dog.

Lie by his Side. Lie in the Path.

Is this the way? Wait for the Day.

Blood. Bitch. Bear.

Axe.

Breast. Bridle. Town.

Knife.

I've come to the edge of the Dark—

a Bee, or Fly

in the Sweetness.

Note:

Vocabulary selected from John Pope's "Catalogue of Indian Words," which he included in the journals, *A Tour Through the Southern and Western Territories of the United States of North-America: the Spanish Dominions of the Mississippi, and the Floridas; the Country of the Creek Nations; and Many Uninhabited Parts* (1792). Pope's brief catalogue begins with the following journal entry (65): June 29th. The *Little King* of the *Broken-Arrow* returned, and furnifhed me with the following Catalogue of *Indian* Words, with a literal Tranflation to each by Mr. *Darifoux*, Linguist to the *Lower Creeks*.

The Maybe-Bird

Hvmken

One week away and the forest has changed

One week away and the forest has changed—
the last version of myself is dying.
My last awareness in the body:
gauzy hands, incandescent willows,
my face in the sediment, declining.
Add a new blanket of earth to the mound—
a hole in time's glove, tear in the sky.
Rainblowers calling to oncoming clouds—
crushed parenthetical shapes of grass,
sublingual camouflaged lanterns.
I envy the unborn, burned gowns
restless in the channel. All I've loved
is a crane's song, half-note in the flood.
The lightness. Language—marvelous thing—
my silhouette, fossil of the drowned town's scroll.

One week away and the forest has changed

One week away and the forest has changed.
Measured wind, consistent in its image.
First frost, day's ghost, chattering red-toothed leaves.
I wander the groves of recycled thoughts,
restless, navigating musty stacks
past gravel tracks, those blushing fields of wheat
golden in autumn's sweep and blossom.
For an instant I turn back and notice
how the glacier, at first sight, is static,
how a train becomes a parabola in snow,
how a swamp tupelo roots in our haze.
To what can we return when we turn time
toward sequence, when we reset the chain
to prove our lives a miracle of flight.
There have been five mass extinctions in our
four hundred billion-year history
and no memory of the formula
for forgetting. What can we make of it
but a hot-air balloon. I wind the key
and wait, suspended against the ruins.

The last version of myself is dying

He told the hunters, drag me in the dirt
and in his wide berth there appeared a lake.
You shaved off his horns, set down your rattle,
disappeared with him into the water.
In this mirror I hunt your debris
of swamp cypress, underwater city—
wake you, singing, from our animal sleep
to return us, twins, to first conception:
engraved carnelian figures in relief.
See the figures lean into the wind
separately, each one a thundering cloud.
When there are two thunders—one real, one false—
which is the original perfected?
The last version of myself is dying.

My last awareness in the body

If it were easy to leave the body
in a breath, as smoke leaves the cupped flame,
rounds itself into a crown and escapes.
Today I fear both the leaving and life,
the accidental step off the world's ledge,
that it might be easy, graceful to go
with my breath like slipping off the saddle
of a faster breathing animal.
My last awareness in the body
was the field upside down, the world a glass bead.
Suspended I was no longer myself—
perhaps I was not anything but sky.
I was not afraid, extending as space,
and felt nothing, no panic, no elation,
my breath neither flat nor curved, bottomless.
What organizes back to the body?
I did not choose my return, or maybe
I became the horse and the horse chose or
simply ran off its spell, shook me free.

Gauzy hands, incandescent willows

I am sitting in the dark theater
alone except for myself on the screen,
my gauzy hands: incandescent willows.
A half-wing, trapped in a fiberglass net,
flaps its other half through the rafters.
Trains cross in and out of the display—
boxcar after boxcar circling the rims
of glass lakes, canyons, tallgrass prairies.
Time can be described as two trains moving
in the opposite direction. As one
recedes to the vanishing point, the other
exceeds the frame—there is never a point
at which one arrives. I try to look away
but return my own gaze by accident
as one might catch, in a window, a woman
removing her wig, her lips, her skin.
Careless, time's mistaken identity—
gazelle spray-painted on corrugated tin.

My face in the sediment, declining

The rails through the forest: noxious black moss.
Our old trails, flint-green, blister with clouds.
Few have come back to recover the dust,
even the rocks are exhausted from waiting—
as if there were still children in the stars,
the moon a shell midden beneath the sea,
her face in the sediment, declining.
We have crossed the fork of the Black Warrior.
We have eaten fish from the hollow tree.
What salted skins were sold for peace of mind
have retreated again underwater.

Add a new blanket of earth to the mound

Add a new blanket of earth to the mound.
Sunflowers blooming from a trashy wash.
Sumpweed, knotweed, pigweed, ragweed, summer's
signature: cenotaph, empty tomb.
The evening veil—a partial reveal—
moon's eagle effigy, winged snake,
eclipse of sun's primordial escape.
I echo the aspen's crack and moan
as winter curls about its throat
to find precision's fitful guise and pine
for lines where swerve the cold, gray streams of lead.
All lines that end undead—not callous, male
or stacked—are rocks where crashed the cyclop's head.
Were sleep to moor like once my mastless boat
in night's dense harbor, fishnets trawling stars.

A hole in time's glove, tear in the sky

I had wanted to return but it was late.
Why return when home is warmed for pain,
where catacombs of dusty vintage weep,
where you are still afloat, late in the hills,
bent cane, crowded head, aflame in dreams
rewritten in English on buffalo skin,
translations for a tone-deaf people.
I had wanted to leave it behind—
this garden of stolen language, planted
in a night that had no story to tell—
to let them believe in your magic. Mine:
a hole in time's glove, a tear in the sky,
what sleeps in a cage at the base of your lung
arranging mosaics of god's face,
a nest of black hair for the birds.

Rainblowers calling to oncoming clouds

Art is an interventionist tool, pure
dialectic, mulberry branch, florum.
Rainblowers calling to oncoming clouds:
thesis, antithesis. I discovered
divination, origin, the reader
inhabiting flaxen flowers of space.
Not telepathy but a verb.
We were clamoring green out of the cane
becoming pictures of calamity.
It is not the anthropocene's membrane
we remember; we resist the image,
resist the resurrection of image.
The only thing moving in the forest
are the spiders crawling out of it and me
weaving at the window the world in its
recurring acts of disappearances
then turning away, turning to the page
to give attention to the firmament,
its flat star charts, seeking art.

Crushed parenthetical shapes of grass

And when the autumn's sweep blows in and turns
tin the churning clouds, catfish trapped in ice
against their own reflection's frozen mood—
bereave their leafy drowning,
brush their pale reflections,
brown the mud, upturn by plow
the crushed parenthetical shapes of grass,
a cloud margin's evergreen signage:
pelofv yomockat se'cehoyarēs.
What detritus, the mind. I wade knee-deep
in eucalyptus leaves, crescent upon crescent's
green effluvient alphabet.

Sublingual camouflaged lanterns

A garden in mid-distillation appears
subject to distortions of perspective.
The winter's orchids, tough pink and chilly—
cruel syntax of a just-cracked iris.
Beaning from existence, frond-tongued tulip.
Your blood on my lips: nasturtiums. What blooms
dusk to noon then sleeps: birds-nest fern, wild yam,
sublingual camouflaged lanterns.
One tarnished star hangs from the catalpa branch
a curriculum for inner vision:
weeping eye, broken heart, bi-lobed arrow.
I swallow the corm. Waiting to forget
this earth, this honey-glanded pitcher plant,
I bury my face in the garden.

I envy the unborn, burned gowns

What lifted when I went through the gates:
a rash of white marsh birds in the meadow,
grassy clatter of antelope. Echo's
wreckage: charcoal teeth, city's unsheathed blade.
How I envied the unborn—burned gowns
gathered in shade—stems snapped, beheaded.
It is nice to be dead like this from grace,
the author of time's bewildering light,
her omniscient inflexible flowers.

Restless in the channel. All I've loved

They closed the subway the afternoon
our boat disappeared over the earth's edge—
a cliff mistaken for dysthymia,
a star's formation as sublime mirage.
When the flood returned to swallow the earth
we hadn't noticed the sky's unblueing—
fish slipped from blackness, flowering sun—
or how hollow the sound left behind—ocean's
flocks tangled in grass. I write under tide
burrowing shut. Soon they will find me
restless in the channel with all I've loved.

Is a crane's song, half-note in the flood

Would she heave her body from these waves?
I was a coral that rattled when shook,
where a snail died inside, its shell left behind.
Bleak, shuttered up, I walk a squid-stained dock,
the long night's confetti dissolving underfoot.
Hand in hand through granular fog, phantom limbs
shift, gargoyles loom from sky's black spires,
tarps thrown over fruit. I duck beneath
a soot-wing's crush, thunder's hushed gallery,
climb its winding stairs, drenched stars' ancient frieze.
By chain-swung lamplight: floating basilicas,
frescoed angels peeling from the ceiling,
salt-print, gum-print, gum-on-platinum print.
My impediment, my not-letting-go
is a crane's song, half-note in the flood.
This, too, is the museum of my blood.

The lightness. Language—marvelous thing

By blood I encountered my formlessness,
hips and coccyx, netting the bones tender.
I was changing from within the deep vein—
a natural death, evolution's echo,
my swallow's fleet, my loom's blue-metered weft
impressed upon the murmuring river.
I had been critical of the music—
the lightness. Language—marvelous thing,
feathered matchcoat of Spanish origin,
flame in my unfashionable closet.
On my crown I can still see the future.
Be mindful, you said. Prepare for change.
I changed the geological record
without past romantic anxiety
because I wanted to understand this
moment in our history: seagulls
hatching from my wrist in full sentences.

My silhouette, fossil of the drowned town's scroll

To be a bride of my own lamentation
I wear a dress not of time's poisoned quills
but feathers of discontent—kingfishers
ghosting in cornstalks, my field of frozen flutes.
The edge of descent, digression's highway
ashes its leftover words in my mouth,
starry metals, meadow's cold snap,
ravens in the scorched black sycamore.
I follow their echo's loop and chase.
I master the map of never, raft
its fragments, mouth the brightness
of goose feather snow, details of a fever-cloud
where the content dissolves in violence.
I become the canyon, its dreaming eye,
lay before the never-returning light
my silhouette, fossil of the drowned town's scroll.

Hokkolen

To be a bride of my own lamentation

I was changing from within the deep vein
into a tree of crimson bark, silvery leaves
trembling in the long dismembered language
of women, scattered into aspirants,
hushed into a breeze. Barely audible
northern moonlight booms from its slow axis.
I could row my boat anywhere from here
to be a bride of my own lamentation.
But my beloved is the water's gaze—
a sheer trough in the center of the lake
that draws me to its bellowing spiral.
In the late dark cloisters of the grotto
my ears skirt the eddy's whirlpooling walls.
A hewn stone stained with rose red seed, the heart
is the inverse of gravity. I listen
for its splash at the bottom of the well.

I wear a dress not of time's poisoned quills

Still I sleep within my two bodies,
a poison, wearing a quill dress of hours
for our dim procession. Each day we wake
to a feedback loop of anoxic oceans.
Were each wave a blank page to begin with.
The sound of my immaterial twin:
the deafening art of repetition,
tinkling rush of shells against the shore's
sculptured mantle, her other self plotting
her reckless escape. Not yet for death,
would she heave her body from these waves?
I become of my two selves the confluence.
When the flood returns to swallow the earth
the day will seem a tranquil derangement.
Most will gather in the interior.
Those left behind will be lost together.

But feathers of discontent—kingfishers

Our beginning was covered in water
and all the animals spoke the same language.
Panther tracked back and forth across the sky's
long escarpments, nightfall and rock mouth.
Buzzard grew tired and flapped his broad wings,
the soil beneath him rippled into hills.
Our threads unraveled. Spider's rains returned.
Beneath the surface of the floodwaters
the lost people rubbed their faces with earth,
their rutted eyes resistant roads of grain.
The only willing survivors—
not ghosts, the planet's oldest organisms—
but feathers of discontent, kingfishers
drifting wind-struck over earth's ancient vents.
Sketched on their city's chipped brass plates
our future's blinking archipelago.
Wouldn't it be preferable to drown,
victims of upperworld explanation?
There are no hard syllables in water.
Our boat disappeared over the earth's edge
and what we didn't see was paradise.

Ghosting in cornstalks, my field of frozen flutes

In my mind's ahistorical era,
a chronology of rivers and trees.
I want to lie down on the road and read
the author of time's bewildering light.
To what purpose—because I believe
the underworld merely an inversion
etched on a gorget, a feathered serpent
ghosting in cornstalks. My field of frozen flutes
hides its motif of interlocking scrolls.
The moon curls into her conch shell and sleeps,
her rabbit-skin shoes waiting on the stoop,
the afterbirth thrown into the thicket.

The edge of descent, digression's highway

To make an apparition, cup your palms
as if catching water. The wind field shifts
what climate has tangled into landscape—
a mind, lost as a white doe in winter,
carcass of anthrax in the permafrost,
a sand's slippage in your hands.
A body's hexed ambition and its shame,
like all geographies of disaster,
are subject to distortions of perspective.
At its edge of descent, digression's highway
will carry the subject to its horizon.
The surfacing image: bent ray of light.
After the wind had cycloned and dispersed
we made a raft by lashing lengths of cane,
bowl-shaped skin-boats with a sapling frame.
Engulfed by the river we did not die
but were drawn down farther beneath the waves.

Ashes its leftover words in my mouth

The singers have fallen asleep in their cars,
small camps smoldering. What they didn't sing
ashes its leftover words in my mouth.
Where are you going? The Sun. The Moon.
Where did you come from? Warrior. Star.
Yet in my doubts I strain to hear
the bubble of salt behind sand snails,
the ocean pulling back into its mouth.
What detritus, the mind. I wade knee-deep
in our stratum's mycelium, laced
like splattered aluminum paint, a mat
of leaves on the forest floor will receive our fall,
we imagined. Before we were forced to leave
we charted the denser galaxies,
trophied the antlers of three trillion trees
to carry with us as a reminder
of the History of the World's End People.
There was no miracle, no other home.
I look to the east, the fire roads.
Marsh birds are lifting from the methane field,
dwarf white roses blooming in my suitcase.

Starry metals, meadow's cold snap

Rainblowers calling for oncoming clouds
are writing constitutions for water.
In this tiny underworld cabinetry
an anxious empire planted its axe.
At removal we are seasoned artists.
The black clouds' incantatory tower
swells—hurricane's cranium splits.
There is still time to learn this medicine,
still time to move the turtles from the road,
starry metals of the meadow's cold snap
patiently waiting for us to return.
Time affords us chaos and collage,
recurring acts of disappearances
through which we can remember our mistakes.
As in: the weather has always been changeful
but we wrote it out of our laws.

Ravens in the scorched black sycamore

Under restless colonial seabirds
we sailed our cargo across the desert
never doubting we could find our way back
to lofty pines, wet glades, creeks of painted rocks.
We carried our dead on cedar litters
until we could carry them no further
then left them by the side of the road
covered in quilts we'd been traded for deer
before the last of the herds were killed off.
Like deer, we could not fathom our escape.
Drew closer together from the flames
only to fall from our hunters' bullets.
Our encampments in the western country
promised us faith and its meager rations.
We waited in line for water and grease
to follow our shadows by gaslight,
ravens in the scorched black sycamore.
To learn the medicine for vanishing
we have eaten fish from the hollow tree,
our ghost now very far from its body.
It travels north and doesn't want to return—
why return when home is warmed for pain
and is anxious to understand nothing.

I follow their echo's loop and chase

Here, where your ghost is always departing
the ebb and flow of terrestrial tides,
I follow your echo's loop and chase,
vortex streets of cylindrical sound
beneath evening's veil, a partial reveal—
how I appear to myself looking past
this fact of being underway. Each day
I stow my earthen materials
in preparation for the never-end.
In the snapshot of my dead friend, hanging
in the room where loved ones refuse return:
a gradual reduction of color.
Running out of time, neck-deep in water
we knew no one was coming to help us
in the same way one denies language
to emerge from a picture. I imagine
love a revelation, not of mind—
the blue gauze of planetary motion—
a tone-on-tone painting of a body
floating on the sea's shifting horizons.
It is a question of legibility.
When I became tired of depicting
poetry, I became aware of
another kind of plane, the kind good

for dwellings and their narrative escape.
Here children sit up all night by the flames—
the orphan boy from blood-stained pottery
who singed his head and burned out both his eyes.
That was your life, a prefix for fire.
Spider will weave a ladder to your heart
it is said, even though you are sleeping,
intoxicated by abandonment,
a bitter wind reminiscent of a wave.

I master the map of never, raft

Bur marigold and cardinal flower:
these are what you should carry to war.
A dried head of the male of the species,
rattles from their hooves, glue from their horns,
deer charms—crystals—in an otter-skin pouch.
Carve your bow of black locust, ash.
Rafts of deerskin to cross the swollen rivers:
bound with grape vines, bundles of cane,
saplings for a keel, ribs and gunnels.
Sometimes instructions return like these,
sea turtles rising from extinction,
dragging their gravid shells under moonlight
as if there were still children in the stars
who were willing to return to us.
This is the point at which I reject poetry
as a solution to melancholy.
In a red-ochered cypress dug-out canoe
I master the map of never, raft
the seven levels of the middle world
from the marshlands to the flat coastal plain
where passenger pigeons blot out the sky.
In forests of towering long-leaf pine
I hear the static of the traveling dead,
the beating of flightless giants, the convent's

whip of waves and seeds. We are two oars
in a dying estuary, shell-heaped
tiers of a burial mound. Each morning's
gray beach of storm petrels and godwits
is a memory, a motionless pose,
a glacier-crushed ship's dismantled ribs of light.

Its fragments, mouth the brightness

You found a small blood clot, wrapped it in leaves
of bitter root, the larynx of the swamp.
You were a singer of untimely things,
crushed sweetleaf and its bloom for insomnia.
Angelica, wormseed, buttonsnake heart
were the stars' gifts, not for us to carry.
You hum your fugue and I follow, leaving
your brackish moss hands in mangroves
asleep beneath the cloak of centuries.
I have tasted the bitters to wake you,
to bring you back into chronology,
but of your lapse I know only to write
its fragments, mouth the brightness of our
storied sky, the calendar we counted by.
Careless, time's mistaken identity
as facing one direction or the other.
Now you are the Maybe-Bird in still grace
perched in the distraction of a forest,
your detachment no more a thievery
than the panther's, who steals a baby from its
dead mother's belly, lays it in a split cane
basket beneath his bed. The universe
is vast but also small and portable.
Some of us are born untethered from time.

Of goose feather snow, details of a fever-cloud

I am tracing from prevailing winds
my breath, neither flat nor curved. Bottomless
is my body resounding with the waves
when there is no sea but abandoned mounds'
old fields' flood plains, indigo-dyed.
A world disembodied is an island
suspended by fraying ropes from the sky,
afloat over thick fog and chaos.
To draw a coastal line in the sand
as a way to understand history
is to hide behind imagination
as if it were a gilded one-eyed mask
through which I can't but pretend to see
goose feather snow, details of a fever-cloud,
oracles of a rainbowed mosaic.
Were the earth to be born from our world—
the atlas, her illegitimate author.
I imagine that we never knew better.
That when we reached the final waters
too big to cross, the sun didn't rise or fall
in any direction that was familiar.

Where the content dissolves in violence

Where the content dissolves in violence
I find myself defending you again.
It was as intended, tar on your hands,
live coal on your head, you were your own thief,
a required god. Even as the world ends
there are two thunders—one real and one false.
Which was the weather beneath your language?
When the fawn returned to the wolf's grave
she strung its bones around her neck and sang.
No, I can't resurrect what never died
nor mourn enough the loss that I allowed.
And it doesn't help to write about it
in false terms, which are the turns of language.
Time out of mind is a star, you said.
Simple. A star in the mind
is dust. That is the breathless measure.

I become the canyon, its dreaming eye

In the last days of my marriage to god
I descended their spiraled library,
relentlessly navigating stacks
of shell-tempered mortuary offerings,
sandstone saws recovered from the caves.
I lingered on history's worn stone steps
to write these things, to recollect myself.
What had I unburied, what had I freed
and what is freedom from the human need
to catalogue and clock our porous lodes.
I gazed, eye's closed, at the moon's cratered walls.
Spiders encircled me, spinning their silks
as I listened to the tuning suspension
of the underground particle colliders
vibrating between silence and motion.
By midnight, saplings had sprouted from my hand.
The clouds dissolved into semi-colons
and I with them, into a new language
of branching gestures, air-born spores. From one
infinitesimal thread, a pattern.
It was my first act of disappearance.
I would return before anyone noticed

poems to be found in the forest, not the mind.
There's a canyon between this version of me
and the shadow on the stairs that is mine.
I became this canyon, its dreaming eye.

Lay before the never-returning light

In the rutting season when acorns fall
wind be in my favor for blood-stained leaves,
to drape across my daughter's autumn coat
a trade cloth of scarlet and indigo.
I lay before the never-returning light
eight deer for one gun, blanket, razor, hoe.
Bones of a lion, horns of a serpent
for shot pouches, garters, sashes and belts.
For one pound of deerskin: fifty bullets,
one ounce vermillion, horncombs, linen.
Two pounds of deerskin for one piece of caddice,
gun powder, striped cotton, flannel, duffel.
Two dead deer, dressed, for four silk kerchiefs.
For silver brooches, ostrich feathers,
ear bobs, saddle, bridal, hatchet,
a hole in time's glove, a tear in the sky,
I traded the forest, empty of deer,
buffalo, beaver, panther, fox—
"We bleed our enemies in such cases
to give them their senses."— ~~Andrew Jackson~~

My silhouette, fossil of the drowned town's scroll

Long ago, in one of many stories
a doe returned as her hunter's wife.
The high forest ringing, her silky thread
ribboned the air into a new weather
and you came to the edge of the visible,
descending the rippling earthen ridges
with baskets of larkspur, violets, lilies.
Mute but not to the slit ears of water:
a half-wing trapped in the fiberglass net
of paradise. Language could not take you there.
Of children the hour's swift current pulled under—
what did it matter, their names were flames.
Re-enter the spiral. Begin again.
What you will see is the absence of sight:
history beyond order, un-sequenced blood,
my silhouette, fossil of the drowned town's scroll.

Tuccēnen

Long ago, in one of many stories

We were clamoring green out of the cane,
rainblowers calling to oncoming clouds.
We followed a path of winding white grass
to waters we found too wide to cross
and came to the edge of the visible
where halflings had trapped in a fiberglass net
bones of a lion, horns of a serpent.
None could cross the lake but two cranes singing
how floods would return to swallow the earth—
the children of thunder, red smoke and shells,
long ago, in one of many stories,
driven like snakes out of canebreaks, swamps.

A doe returned as her hunter's wife

I had fallen back, vengeful, into time,
a doe returned as her hunter's wife.
Hello you burnt pine, death's calligram—
he scribbles with the ash of swamp-lit trees
his measured synecdoche for desire:
the camber of my slim neck on parchment.
Golden in autumn's sweep and blossom,
dry leaves spark from the forest canopy
a spell for becoming untraceable.
You have wasted too many of our coats
I write, then dress him in hide and antlers.
I have turned his pages upon him.
I have dug a pit and caught him in it,
covered him with lightwood knots, burned him
then reserved his bones for resurrection,
lines for a poem: *Hello you burnt pine.*
Poems are to be found in the forest
not the mind, like clean-gnawed femurs of deer
who, stalked by hunters, lure them into caves.

The high forest ringing, her silky thread

A mutant rose's neurotoxin drifts
as in a sail at sea that steals away
rippling, flesh-toned undersides of clouds.
As in falconry, the iced eye blinks blue
upon La Cruz, from where the ship sailed,
blown to the mouth of Apalachicola.
In sight, but at a distance, near the border,
you swore you attained a familiar verse,
the high forest ringing her silky thread.
This is the poem I must not write,
you noted, drawing your vessel to shore.
You shaved off your horns, set down your rattle
and thought you could not write another line.
Time out of mind is a star, you said
and ascended the tributary waters.

Ribboned the air into a new weather

Old Man of Sorrow took flight to the mountain
when the earth was first overcome by floods.
The same comet has appeared from the north
to ribbon the air into a new weather.
I should have written more urgent letters
to the president and his cavalry.
All but one of the horses have been consumed.
In the choked Chattahoochee arteries
fish flash green, belly-up in mercury.
What organizes back to the body?
The world we are about to inhabit
still dreams of gold and virgin planets,
fire, water, locomotion and hope.
But no trace will remain of women,
returned with the drums to the towns underground.
In a stream clear with flowering stones:
the rainbowed mosaic of the oracle.

And you came to the edge of the visible

We were clamoring green out of the cane.
The surface beneath us rippled with time,
with rainblowers calling for oncoming clouds,
for our drowned towns' song, underwater thunder.
We followed the path of winding white grass,
sunned and dried our children on the shore
of the waters we found too wide to cross.
We found a small blood clot, wrapped it in leaves
and came to the edge of the visible
to find our people covered by fog,
a murmur of birds in a fiberglass net,
trailing behind them a ribbon of water,
the bones of a lion, horns of a serpent.
All the animals spoke the same language
but none could cross the lake but two cranes singing
a name to sound the town and its people.
When the flood returns to swallow the earth
those left behind will be lost together.
For thunder, red smoke, the children of shells,
we were named for the Town Lost in Water.
Long ago, in one of many stories
when the earth grew angry and ate up its children,
we were driven like snakes out of canebreaks, swamps,
to re-enter the spiral, to begin again.

Descending the rippling earthen ridges

The rails through the forest: noxious black moss.
A single radiographic image:
my human form against infinity's
cinematic Eden. I am followed
by a watchful subterranean crane.
Descending the rippling earthen ridges,
a burial mound's tetragon terraces,
I hear the static of the traveling dead,
a fin's quick switch that shatters its skin.
My mind moves fast, not in one direction—
a pen's miniature mimeography,
needle on a record, zigzagging pressed sound,
the already bled anxiety of sleep.
I am a scythe in the wheat, wind turbine,
listening for summer's pixilated pine,
the strangling garden of computerized reeds
where nothing material enough occurs
to leave such deep and ruthless tracks as these.

With baskets of larkspur, violets, lilies

We travel his crumbling colonnades
by canoe, me and St. Marie de la Mer,
a scarlet macaw and polar bear
rescued into imaginary light.
We row to rewrite the continent's
eroding edge of unattainable sound—
autumn's chrysalis, the monarch's remains—
and in the enemy's gulf, dig for words:
hay meadow, flower-rich, oilseed rape.
This landscape's quixotic orthography
spells Scipio's spheres, his starbelt of milk,
moon's eagle effigy, winged snake.
It is a question of legibility,
how we appear before we disappear—
with baskets of larkspur, violets, lilies
gathered for an infinite descent.

Mute but not to the slit ears of water

We would reach the end of our trail, they said.
We too have our methods of deception.
Dammed and channeled in the wrong direction,
rivers once, we concealed ourselves in dust.
Invisibility was essential
to tracking over time our reflection,
to gauge the distance a wave could travel.
Mute, but not to the slit ears of water,
we carried our dead on cedar litters,
not in body but in our mourning hymns,
until we found a new town for our fire
and a cenotaph to lay them in.
We left only one story behind us
and a nest of black hair for the birds.

A half-wing trapped in the fiberglass net

Clamoring green out of the cane
we came to the edge of the visible.
Beneath us the surface rippled with time,
our people covered by fog.
Where were the rainblowers, oncoming clouds?
Halflings had trapped in a fiberglass net
our drowned towns' songs, underwater thunder.
Trailing behind us: ribbons of water.
We followed the path of winding white grass
over bones of lions, serpent horns
to a shore where we sunned and dried our children.
We spoke the same language as animals.
But the waters we found too wide to cross
and none could cross the lake but two cranes singing
to make a small blood clot and wrap in leaves
a name to sound the town and its people.

Of paradise. Language could not take you there

The poem had no temporal defense—
abandoned, it fled its historical texts,
crossed mountains, pretending time to pass.
Up and down stairs, in and out of rooms
I write into oblivion going
nowhere—pen runs out, computer dies.
Are we material or electronic?
Or birds of the cross-sea's alliances,
red underwings igniting the wheel
when autumn's sweep blows in and turns
inward the horizon's eyes, its ripped mouth
bleeding out the burden of a forest.
Paradise—language cannot take us there.
Each pass I cross, the same scene reappears:
alongside the atlas's scribbled road
the singers have fallen asleep in their cars,
an errant breeze through the foliage,
their almost imperceptible ascent.

Of children the hour's swift current pulled under

My just-cracked iris, beauty's cruel syntax
blinks from a museum of dead grammar.
I want a breath where there is no body,
to write the sentence of a shifting tide,
a bead for each seagull in the sequence
of children the hour's swift current pulled under.
I want space around the word, just enough
so that its shadow irritates the line—
wind-chime—such expensive equipment
the mind, lost as a white doe in winter.
Butchered once by starving hunters, she would
starve them out for centuries. Her witchery
my looping trail, a crown of prints in snow.

What did it matter, their names were flames

It is nice to be dead like this from grace,
glass door cracked open for breeze,
crows unrolling October's paper curtain—
a scroll across the meadow's lunar slopes
for off-season aeriform alphabets.
I want to lie down on the road and read
the gold-fringed leaves of an autumn diction
yet stand between my two selves, paralyzed,
accounting to do, cooking and email.
Must write the girls to thank them for the wine,
study the dictionary of angels—
what does it matter, their names are flames
and my mind hurts, all night terrorizing
its survivors. Each thief of thought
a phantom word whose oculi stalk me
through every eye. The crush of people
at the departure terminal, pleading
to their gods for the ship that never comes,
still haunts me. Stripped of their belongings
they climbed, limb over limb, skywards,
the words on their tongues no nearer the stars
or the circling birds. A lighthouse beacon
flashes through my window. The end for some
is the body no longer being burdened

to believe. For me, this is where I begin.
I take up my pen in the frigid house,
a pile of feathered bones at the door,
last year's bears asleep beneath the floorboards.

Re-enter the spiral. Begin again

We came to the edge of the visible.
When the flood returned to swallow the earth
we found our people covered by fog—
those left behind, we were lost together.
We listened for songs in our fiberglass nets,
for thunder, red smoke, the children of shells
trailing behind us as ribbons of water.
We were named for the Town Lost in Water,
for bones of a lion, horns of a serpent.
Long ago, in one of many stories,
all the animals spoke the same language,
then the earth grew angry, ate up its children,
and none could cross the lake but two cranes singing.
Driven like a snake from the canebreak—
a name to sound the town and its people.
We entered the spiral. Began again.

What you will see is the absence of sight

The city empties its animaled streets
in a fusion of hydrogen nuclei.
A solar system surfaces in snowmelt
technology's childhood pastoral—
magenta cactus, poppies under storm—
the legal historiography of forgetting.
Forget about the present, it is a
distraction. You will risk losing your dream—
cloud formations at dusk: stack of koi fish,
a swan across the crease of smooth canoes.
Climb the winding stairs, drenched stars' ancient frieze.
As you become of your two selves the confluence
what you will see is the absence of sight:
your body in chalky backscatter,
the violent flattening of difference.

O

History beyond order, un-sequenced blood

Having ingested the valley entire,
calm canals reflecting autumn's trees,
I am cold again, with no radio.
My natural death: evolution's echo,
history beyond order, un-sequenced blood.
I could row my boat anywhere from here,
apprehend the page as an equation,
its environment as it existed
pre-information, a nature poem
off the grid of the cognitive kingdom,
a forest before it was called forest, as in:
I walk along the boardwalk, steel sky, wind,
then trap them in my apartment—the I, the you—
the letters and their feathers—white suited crane, or
red-eyed, surface-diving, oiled Eared Grebe.
Oh Maybe-Bird, what will you name us now?

My silhouette, fossil of the drowned town's scroll

I lay my aloneness in a beast's shrine,
forget what I came for, how I planned
this hour, this day, this life, this time.
The hypnotic racket of the living—
what I wreck against, this cage I made
of silence. Drowned the sound of your retreat
to another flooded beginning,
to the earth's edge, where difference ends.
An image captured for the quickening:
the spiraled staircase of a sundial.
It is not your face in the lake I see—
I find you nowhere that is here or there.
I turn and face the other direction
where horned serpents glitter toward the sun—
a stag in a thicket, linen in the wind,
my silhouette, fossil of the drowned town's scroll.

Osten

I lay my aloneness in the beast's shrine

By blood I encountered my formlessness,
a sheer trough near the center of a lake
where I moor my boat and float in absence
collecting names I had forgotten
or left at the gates when I descended.
Of the upperworld I only remember
a cellar, lit by wisps and lamps, portals
to the sun, its gilded reliquaries,
navigable not by bird-light or moon, her face
concealed behind the stars' dull hatchets.
Where snapped trees breathe with ghost food, moss
I have laid my aloneness in the beast's shrine,
left my footprints on the muddy shoals,
the reflection of myself in water
dispersed by a nervous brushwork of grass.
Oh Maybe-Bird, what will you name me now
disappearing as I am from the body.

Forget what I came for, how I planned

The passage into the interior
is riddled with masks, skins shed, hung for trade.
I row across the mouth of the cenote
forgetting what I came for, what I had planned.
A frescoed angel peels from the ceiling.
What glimmers in this body I bend into:
cracked water moccasin yellow from the sun,
my own face looking back as I drown.
The sound of my immaterial twin:
blue-green marbling of a serpent's coil,
feathered shadows on the concrete wall—
a violent flattening of difference.

This hour, this day, this life, this time

This hour, this day, this life, this time
wasn't meant for us to change the law
written over ancient oyster beds.
Rvro lvstet hvse pvkpakat ohsololotkes mon somkes—
long ago, in one of many stories
a black fish slipped from a flowering sun.
We search aerial photographs for the site,
the drainage of the Coosa river,
its long escarpments, nightfall and rock mouth
constructed as a barrier and door
but the surface is never anything more
than a play of reflections of *other things*:
a people's baggage thrown onto their graves.

The hypnotic racket of the living

Outside the house a woman is dreaming
a scroll across her meadow's lunar slopes.
Her garden in cloud-light is white and black
with soot borne aloft from the northern fires,
the moon's fine clothing being blown away.
I want to turn away from this woman
but to what purpose—because I believe
the hypnotic racket of the living
an absurd attempt to navigate the blur,
the blinding traffic of night's beheading?
He has hidden the sun behind the moon
and covered her face with a bearskin.
With the tails of numerous beavers
he has concealed the twinkling stars.
The stationary flight of a caged bird
is what is said by what's not being said—
I arrange in a vase by the window
her omniscient inflexible flowers.

What I wreck against, this cage I made

I wanted the sentence of a shifting tide.
The blue flirt of hatched clouds. A canyon wren
obscured by snow. The sound of extinction:
cypress cones cracking in the canopy,
parakeets nesting in the hollow tree.
But I cannot language the tree or point out
the surfacing image, its bended light—
your blood on my lips: nasturtiums—what blooms
as inflorescence in the sleeping mouth.
In the solar assembly of twigs and birds,
the damselflies' hindwings, fig's quickened bud,
I awake into thought as you slip from my shore
and nothing I write can draw you back
where daylight casts stark shadows on the page
I wreck against, this cage I made.

Of silence. Drowned the sound of your retreat

It was a double ascension, your body
buried beside a flicker in the sand,
your small camp smoldering. What you didn't sing:
an errant breeze through the foliage,
the green effluvient alphabet of silence
drowning the sound of your retreat
into the violent order of hours
where I lose you by turning to hear you,
the imprint of birdsong in an empty sky.

To another flooded beginning

I have sheared a small lock of hair from each—
the people of coal, the people of clay,
thesis, antithesis—and discovered
one the only antidote for the other.
Loss has allowed me chaos and collage
to imagine each story as discrete,
each gap a prehistoric horizon.
Ours was a deliberate emptiness
not a coincidence of allegory—
how the horned serpent returned to Coosa
trailing behind him a ribbon of water.
He came to retrieve his beloved
and carry her with him under the waves.
Were it not for him, there would be no you,
and you are nowhere retrievable.
Maybe we are all a repeating story,
one that returns to us, the World's End People,
another flooded beginning.

To the earth's edge, where difference ends

Writing from a lone corner of the nation
I no longer recognize the difference
between the name of the wall and the wall
itself. I write a sound without dimension,
an utterance with no one to listen
for the radical aspirated roll
to the earth's edge, where difference ends.
The river has concealed itself in dust.
With the devil's rotting apples and our flags
I arrange a mosaic of god's face.
Exhausted by the work of finding words
which never work, my usual worries:
a synchronized gesture, a closing door.
I have no referent for the polar bend,
the orphic garden, radial descent.
I know life by the blurred periphery
of its passing, as if it were a train or
its caboose—its copper face or tail—
a ghost now very far from its body.

An image captured for the quickening

The turning point came early, bleary-eyed.
Turtle was already ahead of time,
stealing prickly trinkets of lightning,
the night's beaded intertidal chitons.
With first light came first waves of departures—
they folded their fishnets, flutes and arrows,
eclipsed the sun's primordial escape.
We knew no one was coming to help us.
I shielded my daughter from the rain.
All our old objects chained in their places:
the cracked face of a traded timepiece—
how we appear before we disappear,
an image captured for the quickening.
I would become my own coffin, for her
a raft. This was how they found us, after.

The spiraled staircase of a sundial

A Maybe-Bird with no surviving name,
vyomockusan em etēkēn alikis.
Guided by the fragrance of grass
I drink to the green and its afterlife,
I drink from the cups of poisoned bees
whose moon is the midden beneath the sea
of royal comb venus, imperial harp,
whose century's blue curve wheeling toward shore
is a single radiographic image:
the spiraled staircase of a sundial,
a glacier-crushed ship's dismantled ribs of light.

It is not your face in the lake I see

I sit in the darkening theater
of the forest, lake mist thin enough
to conjure your return, the next world's
negative, centrifugal photograph.
The raven crouched on the sycamore branch
reminds me of my temporal assignment:
to find our people covered by fog.
I don't know where to begin, where to look,
wrestled under by a water panther
in the tangled weeds of recurring dreams
as before my execution, I stood
idle, shackled against the shooting wall,
my life not worthy enough for death.
There, suspended in digital screen-light
an uncloaked infant abandoned in the switch.
She hums her fugue and I follow, leaving
your spring-shed, broad-leaved exoskeleton
greased into its cage, crackling with dawn ice:
it is not your face in the lake you see
but electromagnetic generation
of grass of gauze of fossils of trains
of milk of gulls of goose feather snow—
the songs I scribble against deception
to sail through other people's raptures.

I find you nowhere that is here or there

I find you nowhere that is here or there.
Below the sunken Uchee path—iron ore.
The ridge dividing water, veined with it—
pea vine, wiregrass, short-leaf hickory.
Old fields' flood plains, indigo-dyed.
When the woods were dense, saw palmetto,
grapes of the hills destroyed by fire,
the haw chestnut by the hatchet.
If it were easy to leave our bodies
in the fork of Red River, two mounds of earth.
If it were easy to leave you behind
in a stream clear with flowering stones—
to find you in the language where I lost you
as if you were a sentence in this poem
and this poem an archive of the forest.
But I have burned the remaining pine.
On the bluffs, strawberries thinly scattered
and in the old beaver ponds, briar root,
a bread made of it for times of famine.

I turn and face the other direction

I thought I could not write another line.
Simple. A star in the mind
is as far off as I am from being useful,
replacing the shells where I first found them—
whirling spines, turrets, delicate slippers,
engraved absence of the cowrie's black eye.
I turn and face the other direction
to pace dusk's looming promontories,
the dunes' end-of-day embankments, sifting
for lightning whelks' dextral shells,
abalone, sharks' teeth, rare amber pen,
for one sentence of iridescence, one
light-refracted interior word
that will return us.

Where horned serpents glitter toward the sun

Hello you burnt pine, death's calligram.
The war appears to come to no end.
I wander the grove of recycled thoughts,
descend its spiraled library
to seek something louder than the thing
that has no sound by itself, wind in sheets,
the making of silk, not silk itself, not
a silkworm's bitten mulberry leaves
but its synthesis of fibers, proof
of a self that dwells in sound, this poem
beside me, iris in her tomb, silk green
my lover, my sympathetic trapper,
flowering mouth of my vernacular
who opens in autumn under stolen light—
my horned serpent glittering toward the sun.

Stag in a thicket, linen in the wind

In the rutting season when acorns fall
we come to the edge of the visible.
My last awareness in the body:
stag in a thicket, linen in the wind.
Never-ending grass: our punishment.

My silhouette, fossil of the drowned town's scroll

The waiting room where no one waits
opens at the edge of a field. What do you see,
being rowed across, weightless as you are?
The earth suspends its one inky eye.
I peel back the surface of the water:
fish in your blood skimming the blade.
Do names, once they lose their bodies, float?
Memory is not actual weather.
We've already passed through that window—time
is not the passing train but its passage
into absence as we enter the black
stream in the gulf's hypoxic canyon.
There is no one here to speak back—no clock,
no bird, no tree's throatless singing.
Sewn along the spit: spent casks of wind.
Perhaps between the light and its absence
is arrival. There is no other room.
My silhouette, fossil of the drowned town's scroll,
is the glass mind rearranging itself.
Is this the poem I must not write—
this screen upon which I watch the train move
which is itself a moving screen: each pixel
half reflecting my face, half framing
a coral's ghostly taxonomy,

the sea in between concealing its quiet
transition to death: fluorescence, bleach.
The sea will forget everyone—the names
I have kept, names I have banished.
I trace the turquoise curve for a window,
for that vast humming field, its tunneling dark,
where I race against your ghost, where I vanish.

Hvcce uefihnē
nakvhake ocat ēhecē ofvn
pomvculvke tate hecēs.

Notes:

"The Maybe-Bird" is a net.

One line each from poems *o* (from *Hokkolen*), *A* (from *Tuccēnen*), and *XV* (from *Osten*) are spliced into the first poem in *Hvmken*. The second poem in *Hvmken* is made from the first line from the first poem (1/1), as well as a line each from poem *n* (from *Hokkolen*), *B* (from *Tuccēnen*), and *XIV* (from *Osten*). The third poem in *Hvmken* is built from the second line from the first poem (2/1), as well as a line from *m, C,* and *XIII.* The pattern continues in this way. The 16th poem in *Hvmken* is built from the the fifteenth line from the first poem (15/1), and fifteen additional lines. These 16 lines from the 16th poem in *Hvmken* become the primary lines for the 16 poems in *Hokkolen.* This pattern continues in the second, third, and fourth section. Additionally, a four-part spiral poem of a certain pattern is woven through Tuccēnen, comprising the first, fifth, ninth, and thirteenth poem. Finally, a line from each of the "Sixteen Shadows" is spliced into each of the 16 poems of *Osten.*

The choreography for "The Maybe-Bird" is charted in Appendix A.

Coosa: An ancient Mississippian Chiefdom in the Southeast, considered one of the largest.

**"We bleed our enemies in such cases
to give them their senses."—Andrew Jackson.**

Source: Kathryn H. Holland Braund, *Deerskins & Duffels:
The Creek Indian Trade with Anglo-American, 1685-1815.*

All but one of the horses had been consumed

Source: Alvar Nunez Cabeza De Vaca, *Adventures in the Unknown Interior
of America, First Lieutenant in the Nárvez Expedition, 1527-36,* pp.45.

fire water locomotion and hope

Source: Alvar Nunez Cabeza De Vaca, *Adventures in the Unknown Interior
of America: First Lieutenant in the Narváez Expedition, 1527-36.* pp. 54-55:
"Here we made a fire and parched some of our corn. We also found
rain water. The men began to regain their senses, their locomotion, and
their hope."

**Time out of mind is star, you said.
Simple.**

Source: Lucas J. Finnegan, a star in the one mind

" . . . Time out of mind. (Which is perfectly simple.)
I am a lost soul in the dazzling scene.
Or was,
Until I chose to
Come from the place of heart
As the always conscious consciousness
As a star in the one mind."

**Old man of sorrow took flight to the mountain
when the earth was first overcome by floods.
The same comet has appeared . . .**

Source: George Stiggins, *Creek Indian History: A Historical Narrative of the Genealogy, Traditions and Downfall of the Ispocoga or Creek Indian Tribe of Indians by One of the Tribe (1788-1845):*
"So they fled, but only a few of them reached the mountains, most being overtaken and overwhelmed by the waving torrent of water. The 'old man of sorrow' was one among them who escaped by his flight to the mountains. He uttered his wailing and lamentations continually, and in tears of sorrow he mourned for all who perished . . . The earth was overwhelmed by billows of water and no one survived that did not attain the summit of the mountains. From these the earth was repeopled." (43-44)
"The comet was visible during the summer of 1811. The first earthquake shock that convinced the Creeks that Tecumseh has 'put his foot down' came on the night of December 16, 1811. The shock was accompanied by loud subterranean noises." (158)

The surface is never anything more than a play of reflections of
other things

Source: Cesare Pavese, *The Burning Brand, 17th July 1944.*

Below the sunken Uchee path—iron ore.
The ridge dividing water, veined with it—
pea vine, wiregrass, short-leaf hickory.
When the woods were not burnt, saw palmetto,
grapes of the hills destroyed by fire
and the haw chestnut by the hatchet.

. . .

On the bluffs, strawberries thinly scattered
and in old beaver ponds, briar root,
a bread made of it for times of famine.

Source: Erasure and repurposing of text from Benjamin Hawkins's
"Sketch of Creek Country." *The Collected Works of Benjamin Hawkins,
1796-1810* as well as *Travels of William Bartram, edited by Mark Van Doren*

He has hidden the sun behind the moon
and covered her face with bearskin.
With the tails of numerous beavers
has concealed the twinkling stars

Source: John Pope, *A Tour Through the Southern and Western Territories of
the United States of North-America: the Spanish Dominions of the Mississippi,
and the Floridas; the Country of the Creek Nations; and Many Uninhabited
Parts* (1792).

Poem 9 was commissioned for SFMOMA's Open Space project, "147
Minna" (San Francisco, CA, June 2019).

Poem XVI was in part commissioned for Interface Gallery's Creative
Engagement Series with Teresa Baker (Oakland, CA, October 2019).

Translations from Mvskoke:

Nakonakv vcakayis. Hvse ah–ossan
        I follow the story. The sun rising over

uehvtke rakko tempen vlakis.
        the ocean's edge I arrive at.

Vcekelliyat, yopvn ē–oh–hecis:
        I turn back, behind me I see myself:

Nake vcvhakat, cvtorofv vnsekos.
        my image, the face disappears.

★

pelofv yomockat se'cehoyarēs
        in the dark swamp we will find you

★

vyomockusan em etēkēn alikis.
        I go to the edge of the darkness

★

Rvro lvstet hvse pvkpakat ohsololotkes mon somkes.
        The black fish disappears into the flowering sun

★

Hvcce uefihnē
    In the current of the water

nakvhake ocat ēhecē ofvn
    in the image of ourselves that we see

pomvculvke tate hecēs.
    we see our ancestors.

Appendix A:
Choregraphy for "The Maybe Bird"

Hvmken (1-16)

1	2	3	4	5	6	7	8	9	10	11	12	13	14	15	16
	1/1	2/1	3/1	4/1	5/1	6/1	7/1	8/1	9/1	10/1	11/1	12/1	13/1	14/1	15/1
o	n	m	l	k	j	i	h	g	f	e	d	c	b	a	
A	B	C	D	E	F	G	H	I	J	K	L	M	M	O	
XV	XIV	XIII	XII	XI	X	IX	VIII	VII	VI	V	IV	III	II	I	

Hokkolen (a-p)

a	b	c	d	e	f	g	h	i	j	k	l	m	n	o	p
1/16	2/16	3/16	4/16	5/16	6/16	7/16	8/16	9/16	10/16	11/16	12/16	13/16	14/16	15/16	16/16
O	N	M	L	K	J	I	H	G	F	E	D	C	B	A	
I	II	III	IV	V	VI	VII	VIII	IX	X	XI	XII	XIII	XIV	XV	
15	14	13	12	11	10	9	8	7	6	5	4	3	2	1	

Tuccēnen (A-P)

A	B	C	D	E	F	G	H	I	J	K	L	M	N	O	P
1/p	2/p	3/p	4/p	5/p	6/p	7/p	8/p	9/p	10/p	11/p	12/p	13/p	14/p	15/p	16/p
o	n	m	l	k	j	i	h	g	f	e	d	c	b	a	
XV	XIV	XIII	XII	XI	X	IX	VIII	VII	VI	V	IV	III	II	I	
1	2	3	4	5	6	7	8	9	10	11	12	13	14	15	

Osten (I-XVI)
(S = Line from Sixteen Shadows, Poems 1-16)

I	II	III	IV	V	VI	VII	VIII	IX	X	XI	XII	XIII	XIV	XV	XVI
1/P	2/P	3/P	4/P	5/P	6/P	7/P	8/P	9/P	10/P	11/P	12/P	13/P	14/P	15/P	16/P
O	N	M	L	K	J	I	H	G	F	E	D	C	B	A	
a	b	c	d	e	f	g	h	i	j	k	l	m	n	o	
15	14	13	12	11	10	9	8	7	6	5	4	3	2	1	
S1	S2	S3	S4	S5	S6	S7	S8	S9	S10	S11	S12	S13	S14	S15	S16

Acknowledgments

The poems in this collection have been published, sometimes under different titles, in the following journals and anthologies: Cutthroat 26; Water~Stone Review; First American Art; Georgia Review; Hunger Mountain; Kenyon Review; *Living Nations, Living Words*. W.W. Norton, 2021; POETRY; *Native Voices*. Tupelo Press, 2019; Poem-A-Day, Academy of American Poets; Poetry London; Waxwing Literary Journal.

This book is for my family, Janet, Schuyler, and Allyson. Thank you for always being with me.

Mvto to Rosemary McCombs Maxey, for her friendship, laughter, and guidance in the Mvskoke language; Mvto to Joy Harjo-Sapulpa for her mentorship, friendship, and ongoing inspiration; to Eleni Sikelianos, Graham Foust, Bin Ramke, Sonja Kravanja, Ben Estes, and Alan Felsenthal who gave time and attention to these poems; to the shells, sea, and pelicans of the Hermitage Artist Retreat; and to all the teachers along the way and tomorrow.

The Net

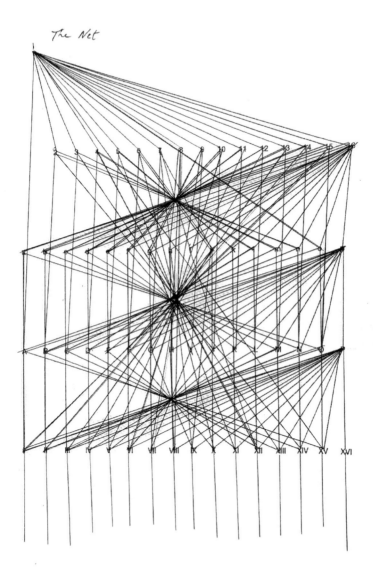

OTHER TITLES FROM THE SONG CAVE: